Come
Home
to
Harmony

Come Home to Harmony

Sharon Hoffman

New Leaf Press

First printing: January 1999

ISBN: 0-89221-473-2
Library of Congress Number: 99-070074

Cover by Janell Robertson
Cover art by Kit Hevron Mahoney   .

Printed in the United States of America.

Dedication

To my mother
Lindy Baird
in whose heart and home I find sweet
comfort!

Thank you.

*They shall not hurt nor destroy in all my
holy mountain: for the earth shall be full of
the knowledge of the Lord, as the waters
cover the sea* (Isa. 11:9).

Acknowledgments

My heart holds dear all the precious ones in my life who have helped to make these pages a reality . . . many thanks from my heart go out:

To my husband, Rob, for giving me daily gifts of love, encouragement, and perspective. The greatest comfort in my life is having you by my side!

To Mindy, Missy, and Mike — how grateful I am to be your mom. You three bring chaos and comfort to my life . . . I love both!

To Dana Grimes for your polished writing contribution, and especially for your sustaining prayer, perseverance, and *pushing*. (You always seem to know when I need the latter!)

To my dear CCBC gals for carving out periods of quiet for me and for being an awesome "test group" for much of this material. Your lives verify God's comfort!

To the New Leaf Press family! You heard my passion and have been great each step of this project. I'm grateful to partner with such a godly, fun-loving team.

To Florence Littauer for your enthusiasm right from the start! You and Marita truly *wanted* me to write this series. You're the best!

To Marabel Morgan, whose teachings when I was just a newly-wed spawned much of my learning for loving my husband and my home.

And to you, dear reader friend, may God truly be the comfort of your heart and of your home.

Introduction

Fastened just above my kitchen sinks are two identical switches. One turns on an overhead light, the other discharges the garbage disposal. While putting together a meal or cleaning up afterwards, I often spin around and flip a switch. What follows more often than not, is an ear-piercing rumble signaling me that my hand truly is quicker than my eye. Everything from glass candle holders to dog collars has been caught in the grip of that disposal and met a perilous fate!

Oh, sure, my intentions are always good. But, blame it on haste, preoccupation, stress, or the sheer fact that I'm blonde . . . inevitably when I want to turn on the light, up goes the switch to the disposal. (I have scores of earrings that don't have mates!)

I think there is a real application here as to how our homes function. Though our intentions start out good, we're on "overload" or too preoccupied or too busy to take notice of what we're reaching for or whose buttons we're pushing. Hurling through depression, divorce, discouragement, disagreements, or death (all of which could hit any of our homes at one time or another), we find ourselves mutilating the feelings of those we love the most. First, our teeth clamp down hard on anyone who gets in the way of our own happiness. Then, click! On goes the "on" button that sucks in, chews up, and noisily disposes of precious ones we love. Like garbage. An empty vacuum in our heart is left behind.

Frightening, isn't it? That scenario doesn't describe at all how I used to play house as a little girl. I loved to dress up in fancy, oversized clothes. To gather my dolls together, all lined up as a family. Using old pie tins and Velveeta boxes, I'd cook on miniature stoves with play dishes. Then I'd corral a neighbor or cousin to be the pretend husband and extended family. My playmates and I would enjoy endless hours of this happy pretend play. After it got late or we'd get hungry and fussy, I'd take my dolls and go home. And the game was over.

Unfortunately, many adults follow the same pattern when constructing a real home. All too soon the "fun and games" is over. Dear friend, it can be better! God has other ideas. He desires our best efforts, but He also provides the perfect blueprint. And a welcome mat besides! God alone can secure the walls of any home so it can withstand even the fiercest of storms. His shelter is essential to build and preserve your home. Get ready for some marvelous building skills!

Join me as we "build" and have an Open House! Through the pages of this book, I'll be throwing open the windows and doors to my home to invite you in. Not to a perfect house, but to an open house, because those that live in it have an open heart. A heart for God. I'm eager for you to meet my loved ones and to tour you through the rooms we come and go in every day.

I'm even more excited to share with you how the storms of disharmony have huffed and puffed and just about blown our house down . . . and how it still stands! The difference between a house and home is right in your heart. Now, come right on in! Make yourself comfortable!

Come Home to Harmony

"Catch-up" in the Kitchen

The kitchen is often called the "heart of the home." Ours certainly is. My family's physical bodies are nourished there. We gather 'round the kitchen table to regroup and refresh. Preparing meals and eating together easily opens the doors for interaction. Many of the most satisfying moments with family and friends have been spent sharing a meal and sweet conversation together.

My kitchen seems to be the room, above all other rooms in our house, that is filled with love and warmth. Comfort reigns. Some of my most treasured conversations with Rob have taken place as we reconnect at the table after a busy day. After-school or midnight snacks provided the perfect occasions in a casual setting to teach Missy and Mindy in their younger years, "line upon line, precept upon precept."

We probably spend more time in our kitchen "funning" and

"fellowshiping" than we do eating. Lingering over a cup of coffee, reading the Sunday paper, finishing homework projects . . . our kitchen is the room that adapts to these many uses. Truly, the real expression of our day-to-day living goes on in our kitchen. In fact, the back door entrance to our home opens right into the kitchen, making it a focal point and hub of our family life.

While we were renovating our house, we addressed the kitchen first because of its prominence. The transformation began to come together when I tried to recall what it is about my favorite restaurant that gives me such pleasure. We then set out to recreate that same

ambiance in our own kitchen/ dining area. We wanted to include plenty of natural light, comfortable seating, and calming colors. It would be uncluttered, useful, yet with decorative touches of charm and character — altogether fashioned in just the right design and atmosphere we had envisioned.

It gives me great

pleasure to know that our kitchen feeds not only bodies, but also replenishes the souls of those who enter. That is my prayer. I desire that all who enter might feel loved and fed emotionally — right down to their soul. Because I personally pass through our kitchen many times a day, I enjoy doing the small gestures that mean so much in keeping the atmosphere conducive to nourishment of the soul.

The best houses have an abundance of heart! That's what instills the spirit of good emotional health. Unpretentious and homey touches can have a deep emotional effect on us. God has created us to respond in our brains to what we see and smell. Fragrant candles, fresh flowers (go ahead, spring for them as you check out the next time at the grocery!), a bowl of sunny lemons to cheer . . . all ideas right at your fingertips! In a kitchen bustling with activity, these small touches of comfort can have an uplifting effect on every member of the family. It's a shame to use them only for company or holidays.

Labors of Love

No matter how modern or conveniently efficient your kitchen is, it is there that you carry out the task of loving others . . . not just cooking for others. If you are a mom, you are teaching many domestic lessons by sheer example. One of the essential ingredients for any home manager is to remember: Good, healthy eating patterns will last the family for a lifetime and pleasurable mealtimes are memories held forever. It is in this way that our grown children never fully leave home. My adult daughters both have homes of their own now but still tell me how certain aromas invoke recollections and warm feelings of home.

Bread dough rising, then baking . . . cinnamon . . . fresh coffee (umm, raspberry chocolate) . . . garlic in homemade spaghetti sauce . . . these are all kitchen scents that trigger my daughters to call long distance. Whatever the season, our kitchen has been a comforting spirit in each of our souls through everyday life. Edith Schaeffer says it well: "The cook in the home has the opportunity to be doing something very real in the area of making good human relationships." The older I get, the more I agree!

Most folks, whether company or family, enter our home through the kitchen door. I see each person who enters my home as someone special. To remind me and them of this, I love to look at my kitchen as a "comfort station." Making a kitchen into a place to lovingly serve helps combat having an attitude of dreaded drudgery. "Better a dry crust with peace and quiet than a house full of feasting, with strife" (Prov. 17:1). You'll be inspired to spend more time there if you perform even the smallest task as "unto the Lord" (Col. 3:23).

Ruth Bell Graham had a sign posted for years above her kitchen sink that read:

Ministry performed here three times a day.

Pouring Cups of Love

I try to remember the above admonition when I feel like dishes are a meaningless drudgery. The choice is yours and mine. We can either choose to resent or to rejoice as we nourish others. Even if the recipients fail to appreciate a sweet attitude, God sees it. It is better to serve a meager meal lovingly, than a banquet where bickering and strife abound (see Prov. 15:17). God always puts it all in perspective, doesn't He? It's not the menu that matters. How it is served and with what *attitude* is what's important!

It's those small acts of care that satisfy my husband more than the "biggies." After a stressful day I love to slip into the kitchen and pour two glasses of Rob's favorite tea. Then maybe I'll place two of his favorite chocolate cookies on a pretty napkin or dish. Pausing to serve my husband in the midst of life's busyness does as much good for me as it does Rob. It sits us still. Quiets our souls. It lets someone dear to me know he is loved and cared for. Those moments of tranquillity uplift us both.

Are there unhealthy relationships in your home

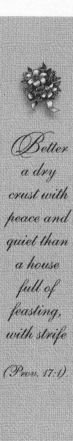

Better a dry crust with peace and quiet than a house full of feasting, with strife

(Prov. 17:1).

Do what you can with what you have where you are.
Theodore Roosevelt (1858-1919)

Neglect not the gift that is in thee, which was given thee by prophecy, with the laying on of the hands of the presbytery
(1 Tim. 4:14;KJV).

that you need to care for? How about dusting off a pretty tray and serving your loved one his or her favorite beverage and sweet treat? Take time to relax and converse together. It takes little effort, but to your family it says they are loved. They will remember the sweet communication and

times shared for years. I once heard that the word "love" could be spelled "t-i-m-e." Spending time one with another is a gift that says "You are loved."

Lovin' in the Oven

A woman in one of my conferences this year wrote me that she "has begun to view her kitchen as the center of her ministry." She used to drag herself into the kitchen each morning and view the room as "functional, yet just a place to perform necessary routines." With two small children constantly vying for her attention, it was difficult for Dorothy to find quiet ways to comfort her husband. She longed to restore the closeness she and Stan had once shared in their marriage.

A month or so after the women's conference a letter arrived at my home. I tore it open and began to read eagerly.

"Dear Sharon . . . dear, *dear* Sharon . . . my *dear, dear, dear!*"

Dorothy had stocked her kitchen with love, not just canned goods! And what a spice it was bringing to her marriage! Her recipe was simple. Instead of always putting the children first and never taking time for Stan, she had begun to work hard on having a sweet spirit in her home. Stan loved sweets on the table, but had told her "he'd rather have a sweet wife than sweets for desert any day!"

Determined to make their home a place of comfort, Dorothy added attractive touches to her kitchen. Simple things like flowers on the table and a candle's glow on the counter did wonders for her own attitude toward this room. She moved a small radio and began to play soothing, inspirational music to set a calm spirit in her own heart. Little note cards with quotes of encouragement and Scripture were placed on the refrigerator and other key areas.

The very first evening after *remodeling* her kitchen, Dorothy came home from work drained. You might know, so did Stan. Still, determined to use her kitchen for ministering to her family, Dorothy prepared a simple, yet delicious dinner. She listened to Stan talking about his day without interruption and preoccupation. He talked and talked. She said he had never talked so much!

"If it hadn't been for the children," she said, "I think he would have thrown me down right there on the kitchen floor! Instead, we put the kids to bed very early!" A change of attitude toward your kitchen changes all sorts of things! Maybe even your love life!

Healthy, Happy, and Hospitable Kitchens

While the primary function of the kitchen is eating, there is no other room in the house where so much goes on that involves the whole family at one time. Keep the following three qualities in mind to make your kitchen *the* place to be:

Healthy — Clean Up Our Act!

Delicious, nutritious meals begin with knowledge of the nutrients that our bodies need and the understanding of good nutrition. Six nutrients that assist in the regulation of body processes have been listed as: carbohydrates, fats, protein, vitamins, minerals, and water. Properly balancing a diet of the foods that contain these nutrients will result in optimum health for your body and mind.

Much work has been done to determine requirements for various age groups and in circumstances of individual needs. I have found that my

A change of attitude toward your kitchen changes all sorts of things!

cooking and my family's eating habits have changed drastically over the last ten years. With numerous health-conscious books and magazines readily available, I am constantly reading more about the importance of nutrition (age, you say?).

Good eating as a lifestyle helps you keep up with an active lifestyle, plus insures defenses against aging. Great beauty tip! I can tell when I have eaten healthy and when I have not. It really shows after I eat junk all weekend or while traveling. Puffiness, darkness under my eyes, weariness . . . just an overall droopy look. When I eat and drink healthy, I look like it! Getting those 8 glasses of water a day makes a big difference alone!

Let children help with food preparation. It makes eating it a lot more fun and teaches good nutrition and cleanliness. You will also find your children more apt to try new foods if they help to prepare them.

Counting fat grams is not all there is to eating healthy. We've all been down the low-fat trail many times . . . and back again. The secret to looking good and living long is to clean up your act . . . your eating act, that is. Clean out all that grease! Low-fat eating used to be low on flavor, too. Today, supermarkets offer such a wide array of fresh produce and aisles full of satisfying, reduced-fat items that make it much easier on the budget and eating habits. This is great news for us snack-a-holics!

Do your body a favor. Learn all you can about healthy foods and

The question is not what a man can scorn, or disparage, or find fault with, but what he can love and value and appreciate.
John Ruskin (1819-1900)

For he saith, I have heard thee in a time accepted, and in the day of salvation have I succoured thee: behold, now is the accepted time; behold, now is the day of salvation
(2 Cor. 6:2;KJV).

adjust old family favorite recipes to new low-fat substitutes. It won't take long before your taste buds start to tingle as you desire a taste for fattier foods. Resist it! As you modify your lifestyle from high in fat to high in health, the rewards are well worth it! You won't *want* to turn back. YOU *CAN* LOOSE THE FAT, BUT KEEP THE FLAVOR! I like to use lemon, herbs, and spices to liven up less flavorful foods instead of adding fats or oils.

"If you replace fat with other more filling, nutrient-dense foods, you can actually lose pounds while eating more," says Annette Natow, R.D., Ph.D., of Nutrition Consultants in Valley Stream, New York. Cheese is one of the most common fat boosters in a woman's diet. Minimize it and choose light-colored varieties like mozzarella, Swiss, and ricotta.

Go for the Green

Brans and grains are not the only source of health. Fresh fruits and seasonal vegetables can add a lot to your decor on the table or counter. I enjoy having them visible. It is not only pleasing to the eye but to the taste as a quick, pick-up snack, as well. It's better than reaching for a chocolate bar or six Oreos!

The bottom line: if health is among your goals for your family, a nutrition-packed kitchen is just the beginning of healthy a lifestyle. Judy Dodd, R.D., former president of the American Dietetic Association and a nutrition adviser says, "There are no *bad foods, only bad eating habits*, which are easy to change if you take things one step at a time."

Happy — Take Time to Smell the Baking

Make your kitchen a room that is so inviting that family and friends (and you!) will want to linger in its welcoming warmth. Your day begins in the kitchen, so start it with items that surround you with joy. If you have to, revolutionize your kitchen with touches that boost your personal happiness. I guess it all comes down to the fact that you can't love others unless you first love yourself. And that would make a great title for a country-western song!

Simplicity Is the Key

Set aside some of those appliances cluttering the countertops. Store them away in low cabinets. Hang a pretty basket or two — or ten. In just five minutes you can "de-junk" your kitchen every day. I know. I have to daily since we enter and drop, enter and drop, enter and . . . well, you get the

You can't love others unless you first love yourself.

idea. Your room will look more spacious and you will be more relaxed while working in a less cluttered area.

Take time in your kitchen to smell the roses — and the baking! I am a breadmaker and my family loves to come home to the oven's fragrance of bread baking. Nothing conjures up the feeling of home's coziness and comfort more than warm bread. Maybe you are not a bread maker. Some women will never be. That's fine. When you do want the wonderful scent, freezer loaves are a simple solution and just as pleasurable as homemade.

Simmering Secrets

Certainly you will find your own sweet smells to fill your kitchen — mouth-watering scents like soup simmering and desserts slipped in the oven during the meal to be served warm. When on days, like recently, there is no time for home cooking, I love to drop a scented wax tart into a small potpourri pot. They come in kitchen fragrances like cinnamon spice, vanilla, pumpkin, cranberry, apple . . . yum, and they last for days. At least that way I have the homey smells coming forth from my kitchen even if there is nothin' in the oven.

Hey, these days, I go by the Hoffman Code of Home Cooking: "If you so much as *buy* a meal within five miles of your home . . . you can call it "homemade!"

Let Your Little Light Shine

Ask yourself if you have a joyful atmosphere in your kitchen. If we want our families to express happy hearts, it has to begin with us. It must be *caught,* not just taught. What a shame that it has become a natural part of many mealtimes to fall into a pattern of sarcasm, complaining, and a time to air frustrations. Everyone leaves the table feeling depressed, rather than with their spirits lifted.

Hold off on the negative concerns until after everyone has a chance to share uplifting conversation. Perhaps the most effective way to bring a relaxing, peaceful mode at mealtime is to make it a habit of inviting God to be present at every meal. By beginning mealtimes with a blessing and thankful prayer, you are helping to turn hearts in the direction of gratitude and peace. Pausing to gather together is a blessing in and of itself. Even a hurried rote-memory blessing is better than none. Our family long ago began the habit of stopping to hold hands, and asks the Lord's blessing on our food and those gathered at every meal.

Let the sun shine in your kitchen with generous doses of the natural

light shining through. Being a "morning person," I like the bright sunshine in the early morning. I've topped windows with a puffed valance, balloon, or swag for a soft effect. I make the most of the sun's rays in our kitchen by using a floral lace for a cottage look. The outdoor view and sun's rays brighten my outlook, is relaxing, and brings the outdoors inside.

Doctors who studied the effect of rooms with outdoor views have found patients less anxious, more energetic, and with higher doses of serotonin — which I understand is a mood-booster that we all could use plenty of! Let the sun shine in!

The way a home is lit will greatly affect its ambiance and comfort. If you are squinting to read the paper at the breakfast counter or to rinse dishes at the sink, you need to lighten up your room. Because the light from overhead fixtures tends to be harsh, I enjoy placing small lamps here and there on my counter tops and window sills. They help to define and add depth to the room.

Similarly, I often use the soft glow of tiny white twinkle lights . . . not just for the holidays. Leave them up in places all through your home all year around. Try twining them around ivy above your kitchen cabinets. What a welcoming sight when you walk in! Use them above windows through garland or to line a shelf. I have strung or tangled them among just about everything — from my fresh flower center-piece to windows to the fixture above the kitchen table for a starry night effect.

Actual lighting fixtures and windows are not the only visual considerations when it comes to lighting your kitchen. YOU become a beacon of light! Don't just let your little self shine — *glow brightly* for all to see!

Hospitality - A Lost Art?

When I am a guest in someone else's home, what I notice most is not what food is served or if their coffee table is dusted or how many pillows are on their sofa. What I *do* remember is genuine kindness, an affirming hug, and a Christ-like joyful spirit that permeates the home.

Having company at your house in the near future? I will be. My kitchen will be a flurry of activity. As hosts, we need to remember the special touches that will help guests feel like family. Your warmth, smile, and welcoming ways will draw others to you and to your faith as you use the gift of hospitality. That's the goal. Not showing off

The best portions of a good man's life is his
little, nameless, unremembered acts of
kindness and love.
William Wordsworth (1770-1850)

Owe no man any thing, but to love one
another: for he that loveth another hath
fulfilled the law
(Rom. 13:8;KJV).

materialistic possessions, but carrying out the admonition of loving and serving others.

In the whirlwind of your life, is hospitality almost a lost art? Let's bring it back! Inviting someone into your home says, "You are important to me and I love you." It can be as simple as a glass of iced tea on the patio or as lavish as a sit-down four-course dinner.

We don't even know the meaning of *that* term at our house, but I have made a habit of using Sunday dinners as opportunities of hospitality. It was those occasions that provided the hands-on training for my daughters to learn the joys of giving others the royal treatment. They both grew up knowing how to set a formal table, serve and refill drinks, and proper table manners by "reaching from the right and serving to the left!"

The key to hospitality is being sensitive to the needs of your guests and offering little extras that say "I care." In those ways we are truly living out 1 Peter 4:9-10 by practicing "hospitality one to another." We must not forget that some have "entertained angels unawares" that God sends our way to give us occasions to prove our compassion toward others.

Be sure not to reserve the spirit of hospitality for guests only. I really believe it should be an attitude in our homes every day; a sharing of our lives with those who know us best and need us the most — our families. The famous 31st chapter of Proverbs is a portrait of a hospitable woman. I want to be a godly woman like her. Hardworking. Hospitable. Industrious. Creative. Best of all, she delights in her role as a wife and mother and is a woman "who fears the Lord."

A woman such as she could put heart into any kitchen! Her reward is that her children arise and call her blessed; and her husband, also, he praises her greatly. Our motivation of loving certainly is not to *get,* but to *give.* Not to expect praise, but to please the Lord. In the process of pouring our lives into others, however, our own cup begins to overflow. I find I am filled and not as hungry for compliments or praise as I once was. Not that affirmation is not nice, but if I am pleasing God in proper motivation, I have deep satisfaction.

It's interesting that the word "hospitality" is wedged in my dictionary between "hospice," a place of shelter, and "hospital," a place of healing. Your dear home today can be that kind of retreat . . . a refuge where you are not seeking gratification, but a sanctuary where healing and shelter are offered to all who enter. Great satisfaction will naturally follow.

I have a dear prayer partner friend who has a special flair for this sort of thing with boundless energy. Her home is a constant source of entertaining. Liz loves to celebrate others' birthdays, afternoon teas, and holiday gatherings. She is not simply paying a social obligation, but is giving different people in our church an opportunity to relax and have a good time sharing their lives together as Christians. Liz has made a great contribution toward strengthening friendships in the body of Christ. I love going to her home. I come away feeling so loved!

Unexpected company coming? I seem to get that memo often lately and have learned a couple of quick cleaning tips that work. Run over the toilet, sink, counters, and faucets with a baby wipe. You're ready for visitors. In fact, having a friend over, even if just for coffee once a week, or a Bible study in your home inspires you (*forces me!*) to keep your home presentable. I keep my house presentable better if I have goals to shoot for.

Living in the Fast Food Lane!

You know how it is. From the moment the alarm rings in the morning, you are off and running. You make coffee, take a quick shower, get kids roused, dressed, and fed. Then it's get dressed and dash to work, spending eight hours or more on the job. After picking up your son at softball practice, dropping your daughter off at soccer, fixing dinner, and helping children with homework, you wind up doing paperwork before tomorrow's

In the process of pouring our lives into others our own cup begins to overflow.

meeting. Whew! No wonder many women have the "5:30 Syndrome." We're frazzled, fussy, and faint! Suppertime follows, resembling a Chinese fire drill!

What motivates me is having a *PLAN*. I can work my plan and take great pride in my accomplishment. Without a plan, homemaking is just a daily grind. There is neither excitement nor fulfillment, much less a pride of performance on the job. It's just the same ol' same ol'. By paying attention to the following details in a simple plan any home can become a more healthy, pleasant place in which to be.

Following a plan is the secret in learning to do things the easiest, most pleasurable way possible! The number one reason I hear women say they do not like to cook is because they dislike the planning and shopping. One way to simplify menus for your family is to repeat the basic main entree every two weeks. Jot down five week-night supper meals and weekend meals that your family eats at home. Keep it simple.

Then, before going to the grocery store, you will know which week's list of items you need to take. The staples basically repeat every two weeks.

One main reason so many families drive through a fast-food is because they fail to plan. After a long, hectic day at the office or at home, who wants to drag in the front door and hear "What's for dinner?" One more decision sends us into overload! So, we end up serving unprepared, unappetizing meals with little nutritional value.

Planning will make your life much, much simpler. I spent too many years *not* doing "all things decently and in order" (1 Cor. 14:40). I am living proof that you can change! "A place for everything and everything in its place" the old adage goes. For the most part, yes, even as we begin the 21st century, duties of managing a home fall squarely on the shoulders of the woman of the house.

Women from countries literally all over the world have reported to me the awesome differences in their households when they began applying the "Twenty-Five Thousand Dollar Plan." I learned the principles of this plan as a newly married years ago in the seventies' "total woman" classes. They still work as well for me now as they did as a newlywed.

It's the plan that management consultant Ivy Lee suggested to his CEO many years ago. He received $25,000 for suggesting this plan to the president of his company. The principles work when applied to household management as well. And believe me, it is worth every cent! No longer will you feel swamped with all you are juggling. You will be calmer, unrushed, and be able to *find the things you need when you need them!*

The Twenty-Five Thousand Dollar Plan

1. Every night write down the important things you need to accomplish the next day.

2. Number them in order as to importance (i.e., dental appointment, vacuum, etc.)

3. The next day, finish as much on your plan as is realistically possible. Do hardest tasks first.

4. When interruptions come, accept them, then go right on finishing each item.

Be realistic. Remember, our goal here is to *simplify*, not cause additional stress. The answer to disorderliness is not vacuuming four times a day or hourly running around the house with a feather duster. Fastidious "neatness neurotics" like that are killing themselves to keep up. (Then there are those of us who have had *Good Housekeeping* or *Better Homes and Gardens* threaten to cancel our magazine subscriptions!)

The best things are nearest: breath in your
nostrils, light in your eyes, flowers at your
feet, duties at your hand, the path of God
just before you.
Robert Louis Balfour Stevenson (1850-1894)

If I take the wings of the morning, and
dwell in the uttermost parts of the sea;
Even there shall thy hand lead me, and
thy right hand shall hold me
(Ps. 138:9-10;KJV).

Tackling Time Enemies

Balance is the key. Too much structure can be just as frustrating as being haphazard. But, if you're like me, I find time is much too valuable a commodity to waste precious energy looking for misplaced items or having many unfinished projects lying around.

Plan. Do your countertops, tables, and desk stay cluttered? How about your closets and clothing? Are you readily able to put your hands on important papers and bills right away? Do you have a will and insurance documents in a protected place? Are you prompt to appointments and work? Is your attire matched, pressed, and shoes shined? Are you a time waster . . . phone talker . . . TV addict? Do you have to be in a hurry to get anywhere on time?

Ugh . . . I'm stepping on my own toes here. Instead of getting over-loaded, let's admit what our individual areas are that need attention. For two weeks faithfully use the Twenty-Five Thousand Dollar Plan and watch your calendar begin to be your friend rather than your worst enemy. Pace yourself.

Do not put on tomorrow's plan everything you should have been doing for the last six months. "Spring Cleaning" is not one point on your list. Too many targets will frustrate you. Remember, simplify . . . simplify . . . simplify!

Streamlining Your Work

Start today! Commitment is the significant ingredient that will motivate you to move from the pitfalls that trip you up and impede progress. Instead of procrastinating, begin today. *Plan. Prioritize. Progress. Pray.*

Prioritize. God puts high priority on organization and orderliness. Proverbs 24:30-34 describes the inefficient person as a "sluggard." "Decently and in order" is our goal!

The point is, when I did not organize my time, my chores ran me. I thought a schedule would be arbitrary and restrictive, but it turned out to be quite freeing. God is a God of order. He is able to use us and our talents best in an orderly fashion. If order is going to prevail in your home, at some point *you* are going to have to impose it.

Progress. Each woman's schedule must be tailored to her individual needs and the needs of her family. A new baby, children leaving home, extended illnesses, etc. obviously mean drastic alterations in the schedule. I find that at least once a year I must fine-tune my schedule. At the present, I have been using a "homemade" priority planner with dividers to mark each section. For years I frustrated myself with those pre-put-together notebooks, so I ended up making my own. In a small 3-ring binder I made my own tabs for sections that applied to my personal calendar, "to-do's," and lifestyle. No two women's lives are identical, neither should their planners have to be! Your own notebook will become a lifesaving organizer, reminder, and reflection of your individual life routines, as mine has.

Pray. Be sure to keep your life message in focus, regardless of what chores seem to be beckoning. Many things just don't need doing *today!* Rob's mother was a great housekeeper and taught me many wise housekeeping "tricks of the trade" during the years we lived near them in Florida. As a frustrated new mom, I wailed my woes to her about everything I thought needed attention. She helped me take a fresh look at my standards. They were too high.

"You don't have to have your kitchen floor clean enough for someone to eat off of. No one is going to!" That advice suited me and has greatly helped me keep perspective down through the years. It's okay to have toddler fingerprints on the sliding door, they can go nicely for weeks between cleaning. Likewise, having two daughters as apprentice homemakers has also served as a great means for delegation, thus lightening my load.

Enlisting Help When Drowning

I am thankful that Rob does not feel his masculinity is endangered nor his role of manliness threatened by helping with household responsibilities. Not long after we were married, we both fell naturally into performing certain tasks that suited us both. Our aim has always been to lighten each other's load, depending on the circumstances. When I was up during the night nursing babies, he handled a tremendous range of cooking, shopping, and cleaning.

Down through the years Rob would take the kids out somewhere in the evening just so I could have an hour or so to give the house a good once-over without interruptions.

As your children get older, make cleaning a family affair. Missy, Mindy, and I could do our heavy cleaning once a week and be done in half an hour. This was attainable because they each had a check list of light chores they needed to get done shortly after breakfast each morning. Because of this, housework did not consume all our time and energy. We started out years ago with those great

Keep your life message in focus, regardless of what chores seem to be beckoning.

chore charts from Current and they loved the accomplishment stickers. I've been in homes recently where they are hanging in full view like ours did from the refrigerator door.

There are numerous sources of affordable, available, outside help when needed. Call a high school or college-age student anxious to earn some extra cash. I cannot get through the holidays or heavily scheduled speaking engagement weeks without it! Form a co-op with friends or neighbors to trade jobs you detest or cannot physically do.

Turn the Tables

Maybe you would be willing to trade some baby-sitting for a friend's help on roofing or building a deck. A friend of mine does great wallpapering for trade-offs that benefit her. I enjoy splitting perennials in my garden and have even planted them in friends' yards in exchange for back-breaking jobs I cannot

handle like painting or shampooing rugs.

Now that we're empty-nesting, rather than clean all on one day, Rob and I have a schedule of a few household chores that get done on certain days of the week. I know no one is going to come through giving a white glove test so I try to remind myself that *people are more important than things.* On crazy days when nothing gets done, I can at least say to myself, "I threw in a load of whites today." I feel very strongly that it is better to spend a day with a hurting friend than it is to get certain chores done just because "it's my day to do them."

Good stewardship of our time often means delaying what can be done later. Chores are incidental to what's really important in our lives. One of my personal mentors the last few years, Florence Littauer, puts it well: "One of the quickest ways to gain perspective is to ask yourself, 'Is this going to make a difference two years down the line?' Inevitably, your answer will help clarify and redefine your priorities."

What is your perspective on scheduling? In her book, *Confessions of an Organized Housewife,* Deniece Schofield says, "You first decide how much time you can or want to spend cleaning."[1] It comes down to balance. I know when I'm focusing on all the responsibilities but not seeing the joys of life. My body always reminds me that I have been pushing too hard. A sore throat and severe case of sinusitis lets me know I need to remedy the burnout. There's only one way.

Cheerfulness keeps up a kind of daylight in the mind and fills it with a steady and perpetual serenity.
Joseph Addison (1672-1719)

Happy is he that hath the God of Jacob for his help, whose hope is in the Lord his God
(Ps. 146:5;KJV).

Mealtime Memories

You can build memories in your kitchen. Mealtime is traditionally a time for family to gather and share their lives together. You can instill the importance of making mealtime an opportunity for your family members to "connect," rather than hastily devouring unappealing, unplanned victuals on the run.

Families' hectic schedules have almost made the "dinner hour" a thing of the past. The effort it takes to bring it back into your home is worth the effort! Expect some resistance from each family member when you unplug the phone, turn off the TV, and *sit* down together for the supper meal . . . as often as possible. Maybe you can't *every* night, but you could once a week.

A spirit of comfort is fostered when you set the stage with a creatively set table and healthy foods that are pleasing to the eye as well as the tastebuds. You will send a message by these gestures that heighten the anticipation of the meal. Any dish just tastes better when served in an attractive way. It also sends a message of care that you want mealtime to be a delicious time for the body *and* the soul.

I'm criss-crossing the country encouraging women to set aside one night as family night, especially at mealtime. As often as you can, share mealtime together as a family. Find what works for your household. Women who have embarked on this undertaking are reporting great improvements in communication and sharing in their families. I know it takes resolve, cooperation, and perhaps some juggling of schedules, especially if you have teenagers. But, you could try it once a week, if not every evening. The benefits and sweet memories are far-reaching! If you don't believe that, ask any lonely teen today. They will tell you they'd gladly give up anything (yes, even sports!) if they could have had close family ties and dinners together while growing up.

Many women now are sharing with me that in their own families, they've made suppertime a time of joyous sharing and family fun!

Bubbles, Bath and Bible

Fifteen minutes a day scheduled in your daily planner *just for yourself* will help you renew emotionally, physically, and spiritually. One day I was able to pay a visit to a horse stable where some of the race horses were worth thousands of dollars. Their stalls were completely padded to guard against any infection from little scrapes and bumps. How much more should we as God's women guard our inner chambers! We can easily become bruised and scraped by this world's everyday problems. Renewing the soul keeps our inner self orderly and beautiful, whether the outer circumference is or not.

Honor yourself today with a time of sheer comfort. Find a relaxing treat that is low in fat content and high in inspirational value. It will put pep in your step! It could be a bathtub. It might be a lawn chair. Relax and read. The Bible is not only *for* you but *about* you. Let yourself imagine how God is comforting you. He is, with His dear nail-scarred hands.

When you want to feel anew . . . take some time for YOU! You can't have one without the other.

When There Aren't Enough Bathrooms in the House!

Whatever else might be said about home, it is the number one place I long to be when I have been on the road traveling for very long at all. Home. It's where I belong. Where comfort holds me in its warm embrace. No price tag can measure its value to me and my family. I'm learning that it is not the comfort situations that bring out the depth of what home means to me, but often the difficult ones. B.J. Thomas belts out the lyrics to the song titled, "Home Where I Belong." You've heard it, and if you're of my generation, probably even sung along:

Renewing the soul keeps our inner self orderly and beautiful.

When I'm feelin' lonely and when I'm feelin' blue,
It's such a joy to know that I am only passin' through.
I'm headed home. Goin' home, where I belong.

True, overall comfort reigns in our home. The last thing I want you to picture, however, is that ours is a Norman Rockwell picture-perfect family that has it "all-together." I don't think that even exists except in art! We, just like you and your family, occasionally get irritable, fall apart, and fail one other. Some days our home has been a great place to visit . . . but, I wouldn't want to live there.

Like when our house only had one bathroom, a mom, a dad, and two girls who were entering their teens. Every morning became an exercise in patience and endurance. Rob was patient and I endured.

For an hour every morning and every night, I endured.

You see, living in a house with one bathroom really encouraged our "family togetherness." Or should I say, *discouraged* it. It seems that Missy absolutely *could not* brush her hair or teeth if Mindy was standing anywhere within 50 feet of her! No matter that the mirror extended the full length of the bathroom wall. The wailing and gnashing of teeth could be heard as far as the driveway.

"She's looking at me!" I recognized the voice as Missy.

"I am *not!* My eyes are straight ahead!" Mindy would retort back for whoever was listening. After repeated warnings and many frustrating mornings, a bathroom time schedule saved my sanity. I marvel now at how well both girls get along. I enjoyed hearing them giggle and gaggle while they were both home visiting for the holidays this year. They love to spend time together. Even in front of the same mirror!

We are constantly filing away at the rough edges. One thing I have learned over the years is that even with three bathrooms now, no home is ever going to be problem-free. There is no one-two-three, quickie formula for the questions homes are facing. During the tough times we will either grow stronger or grow apart.

Before You Blow Up in Anger

Sometimes sheer perseverance is all you might have going for you. Use it! Perseverance can be the mortar holding a home together when we allow walls to build up. Stress and anger are two of the most common "discomfort" walls. Both can be a double-edged sword. Both can be beneficial and can be destructive. They can prevent tragedy or

I wonder many times that ever a child of God should have a sad heart, considering what the Lord is preparing for him.
Samuel Rutherford (1600-1661)

But as it is written, Eye hath not seen, nor ear heard, neither have entered into the heart of man, the things which God hath prepared for them that love him
(1 Cor. 2:9;KJV).

cause travail. The first is usually a protective response, such as if you step into the path of an oncoming car. Stress and fear force you to jump out of the way, preventing disaster. Destruction comes if you allow the stress level to accumulate off the stress chart without intervening. Weigh the options.

Anger is often the result of stress overload. When I put too many plugs into my circuit breaker, there is overload and eventually, burn-out. A total shut-down. If the system did not shut down, my house could catch on fire, causing total disaster.

As humans, we are much the same way. An overload of responsibilities and stress turns up the heat . . . boiling anger results.

Anger has become a way of life for many women, especially under the stress that parenting brings. Fears and concerns that moms 20 years ago did not even have to consider, now dominate daily thinking of mothers. Day care, guilt, kidnapping, deprived needs, abuse, resentments toward jobs or spouses, housekeeping needs . . . all can add up to intense discomfort.

These do not need to control you, however. The root is usually a displeasing situation that has made us bitter, resentful, or hostile — that's when it becomes anger.

Once you better understand the root of your anger, you can find practical ways to diffuse it. In "Steam Mad" by Jill Richardson[2] several ways include:

PLAN AHEAD: Before conflict arises, talk with your children about the consequences of breaking rules.

BE REASONABLE: Don't drag hungry, tired kids on a dozen errands. Recognize when you are demanding too much.

GET EVEN: Don't yell about crackers on the carpet. Insist that the child clean up her own mess. Actions have consequences.

CHOOSE YOUR BATTLES: Seat belts are non-negotiable. (So what if your preschooler wants to wear her swimsuit in the bathtub.)

STOP YELLING: A parent's angry outburst can fuel a child's aggressiveness.

RESPOND IMMEDIATELY: If you don't, the child will keep pushing the boundaries and then you'll explode. If you are boiling over, take five and make your child do the same. Then deal calmly but firmly with the transgressor.

LIGHTEN UP: Start a whining contest with a fussy child. Tickle a complainer till he has to laugh! (I've tried this one and I love it!)

Those are terrific ways to control anger with children. There is an old Latin proverb, "He who goes angry to bed has the devil for a bedfellow." Yes, there are many irritations in life. But, "A fool gives full

*A man travels the world over in search of
what he needs and returns home to find it.*
George Moore (1852-1933)

*And he arose, and came to his father. But
when he was yet a great way off, his father
saw him, and had compassion, and ran, and
fell on his neck, and kissed him*
(Luke 15:20;KJV).

vent to his anger, but a wise man keeps himself under control" (Prov. 29:11).

Home Extension Rooms — The Garden

I love to sit on the deck just outside our back door that overlooks our backyard flower garden, the way I did just today. It is peaceful and serene, forcing me to write about the things God is doing in my life. On a post near the garden's entrance hangs a sign that reads "Love Grows Here." Pausing to ponder between paragraphs today, I realized what an impact that saying has.

No matter where I am or what I am, all that is required of me is to love. To be and do what I am supposed to be and do; but to always LOVE to the very best of my ability.

Today the late summer heat has made the leaves droop. Our scorching Iowa winds have blown over the tall, withering sunflower and hollyhock stalks. Without a drenching soon, they'll never make it.

I walk over to drag the hose in place. The cool nourishment soothes my soul as much as it revives the soil. My garden is an extension of our house — a room out of doors. It is perhaps my favorite room "in" our house. Maybe that's why I spend so much time there. In those quiet times I am free to withdraw from life's demands. In the silence of digging with a hoe or just wandering and listening . . . many of my dreams are born.

From Weeds to Wildflowers

My garden reaches far beyond the confines of its fragrant, colorful walls. That's the way a garden works! In 27 years of gardening, I have learned some healthy lessons there. I started out with six scrawny petunia plants around the tiny patio in our first apartment. Now, flower beds encircle our entire yard on all four sides. Lots of learning . . . lots of growing . . . lots of waiting.

In the classroom of my garden, I have learned a lot about my role as a mother. I'm to plant seeds in my daughters' lives. I then mulch, weed, water, and feed. Past that, the rest of their nurturing is up to God. With the most tender care and preparation on the part of parents, the time comes early when we must also begin to let go.

To plant a garden you can go to the garden center and buy two dozen tulip bulbs. You have prepared the bed removing obstacles that might obstruct growth. You place the bulbs in the soil bed. Cover and bed them down securely. Mulch. Feed. Weed. Water. WAIT. An entire season of waiting is important. Then and only then, do you reap a bountiful harvest.

Effective parenting follows the same sequence. There is no greater value in good parenting than the wisdom of waiting. Gardening helps us all to learn this patience. You just can't rush the growing process — in the garden or in your child's life. The tricky part is knowing how much fertilizer, digging, tending, and pruning to impose.

There is just no rushing flowers . . . or children. I once made the mistake of trying to force some garden blooms to open in time for a garden party. After a cool spring my roses, columbine, iris, and peonies were not at the stage I'd hoped they would be in time for our church Ladies Night Out group to gather on the lawn. I fertilized and watered. I pruned and prodded! To no avail . . . in spite of these extra efforts most buds had not had time to bloom. The results were out of my hands. Even with all this over-nourishing.

Similarly, I've been just as unfair with Missy and Mindy before. I've prodded, pushed, and prompted in times when what they have needed is my patience. Every child has his or her own individual time to bloom emotionally, as well as physically. There can be no comparing. No rushing. Each is one-of-a-kind with a timetable of her own! Beginning in toddlerhood, we parents need to gradually let our child make the transition from parental control to self-control. This gives a child the confidence and empowerment to enter teen years and adulthood.

I have watched the face of my friend Teresa's daughter light up in confidence when given the responsibility to make her own decisions. If little preschooler Ashlyn can only take one toy with her, Teresa says, "You decide." And Ashlyn does. She is being allowed to make a choice of her own and live with the consequences. Teresa is a terrific mother. What a wonderful way to teach responsibility at any age!

Terrific But Specific

Florence Littauer, a dear friend and personal mentor of mine, has written a super book entitled *Silver Boxes.* She clearly shares how we all can be encouragers in positive speech to others. In her effervescent, practical style Florence shares that parents must be especially conscious to use words that build up and not tear down. "We must train ourselves to think before we speak. Once the words are out, we can't stuff them back in — they are intangible, illusive." (From p. 30, *The Gift of Encouraging Words.*)

Speech needs to be as Ephesians 4:29 tells us:

You just can't rush the growing process — in the garden or in your child's life.

*A palace without affection is a poor hovel,
and the meanest hut with love in it is a palace
for the soul.*
Robert Green Ingersoll (1833-1899)

*For thus saith the Lord God of Israel, The
barrel of meal shall not waste, neither shall
the cruse of oil fail, until the day that the Lord
sendeth rain upon the earth*
(1 Kings 17:14;KJV).

"Do not let any unwholesome talk come out of your mouths, but only what is helpful for building others up according to their needs, that it may benefit those who listen." Wholesome speech encourages! Verse 32 goes on to say, "Be kind and compassionate to one another, forgiving each other, just as in Christ God forgave you."

Growing a Bumper Crop

In my garden I am the facilitator, the helper. God is the true gardener. It is because of His creativity and timing that I can triumphantly pick beautiful bouquets in bounty. As the parents of Missy and Mindy, Rob and I both acknowledge, "Every good and perfect gift is from above" (James 1:17). We dare not revel or take credit for their sweet lives. We may hold the trowel and shovel, but we know who is really behind their successes.

Your child has great worth and value. Let them know you feel that they do! I still remember a song named "Sugartime" we used to sing while riding the tractor on my grandparents' farm: "Sugar in the mornin', sugar in the evenin', sugar at suppertime. Be my little sugar and love me all the time!" We can take a lesson from this little jingle. May our words and actions be sweet!

Many authors have compared children to plants growing in the garden of life. Isn't it interesting today that gardeners talk to their plants and even leave music on in their homes to make them grow? If horticulturists talk to their plants to aid in healthy growth, how about trying it with your kids?

Sweetness . . . kindness . . . comfort . . . any time of the day!

How Do You Spell Love?

It takes time — lots of it — to cultivate a comforting climate in which children can grow. Resolve now to give the time your child needs, for "love" is actually spelled "T-I-M-E" to a child. Years ago I received a great garden tip from a seasoned gardener. He stressed to me the importance of checking my garden daily — first thing in the morning. That way, such problems as weed and pest invasions or dry areas can be spotted while they are still small and only take a small amount of time and effort to remedy.

Just like my garden plants, it takes time DAILY to raise a healthy, happy child. In the morning, in the evening, suppertime . . . sugar all the time. Sugar for little tummies is discouraged. But, sweetness from a mother's heart is highly recommended!

IN THE MORNING: Henry Ward Beecher said, "The first hour of the morning is the rudder of the day." I go even further. I'm convinced that the first four minutes the family is together sets the tone for the day! Try to hug and hold — no matter how old your child is — your children in the morning. Even if it's a quick squeeze as they dash out the door.

Oh, yes, they will tell you that they've "outgrown that sort of thing." If you are not in the habit, they will pull away wailing, "Oh, Mom!" Then, about the third morning when you fail to hug or kiss them goodbye, they will seek YOU out first! Parents who withhold touch are not meeting a vital need and are depriving their children of the security of feeling wanted and loved. A girl, especially, will go looking for the stroking she needs, if she does not receive it at home.

Psychologists urge parents to keep on hugging, keep on roughhousing with their kids even into the teen years. They state the reason for rampant teen sex may not be that kids want a sexual relationship as much as they just need to be held.

One morning when the girls were still at home, I awoke exhausted from being up late the night before. I trudged into the kitchen and made coffee. Mindy padded in and watched me making my breakfast in my foggy state. I hadn't even acknowledged she was in the room. About to leave for work and tired of being ignored, she moaned,

It takes time — lots of it — to cultivate a comforting climate in which children can grow.

"Well, I guess I'm leaving now. . . ." She was hinting, something's missing! She knew I'd kiss and hug her goodbye and tell her I love her. Today, even though she's a grown woman, she still needs to be hugged and held.

IN THE AFTERNOON: Plants in my garden wilt in the hot afternoon sun of a summer day. They aren't very pretty or healthy-looking in that state. I don't go out there and start spading them all out of the ground tossing the plants onto the compost pile. I am confident that with some wise watering and "cooling off" time they'll burst forth again in full bloom.

A child needs to know he is not going to be yanked out of the garden and tossed aside when he wilts in the scorching heat of life. Love your sons and daughters unconditionally. Let them know you do. Not just when they are good. But, especially when they are not.

The story is told of a Mrs. Taylor's son who was arrested on a drug charge. The next day Mrs. Taylor put in for time off from work to accompany her son to court. An associate overheard her talking about the incident and remarked, "If he were my son, I'd kick him out!"

"If he were your son, I'd kick him out, too. But, he's not; he's mine," Mrs. Taylor shot back.

My daughters know that I'll never stop loving them — no matter what! Of course, I do not condone every decision they make or approve of everything they do. But, it doesn't affect my relationship with them. They know they aren't loved by what their actions are, but because of who they are. They are mine and Rob's daughters. We love them dearly . . . unconditionally. That holds us together when we become temporarily fragmented in stress or when distances separate us.

A child's feeling of worth is transmitted from his parents by acts of hugging, loving, praising, and accepting. Praise encourages and does wonders to help a child develop his or her special abilities.

A young woman tearfully told me, "My parents never said they loved me just because I'm me. I always had to do and be what they wanted. In fact, they even told me I was unwanted, a shameful "mistake." I have tried every way and every guy I know to find love."

How sad! Can you imagine what that did to her self-esteem? On the other hand, the mother who tells her child, "I believe in you. You can do it, I know you can!" conveys a message of love and confidence. If the youngster fails, he knows he is still loved. He dares to believe in himself. And that's a giant step for a little person to take!

IN THE EVENING: Gardeners like my friends Carmen and Bruce, who have an acreage garden, don't just plant a seedling and forget it, hoping it will come up every spring with no maintenance. Even perennials take work. They have learned by experience how to prevent plants from wilting or weakening and how to rid them of disease and other problems. By evening there is a list of caring tasks still to be done.

Evening is an ideal time to spend loving your children. My girls used to enjoy the family bedtime rituals. "Who doesn't like delaying bedtime?" you say. I was always the one ready to hit the sack first since I'm more of a morning person. But, I am convinced that the energy and commitment it took to make bedtime memorable was *well worth it!*

What a better place this world would be if homes everywhere had parents who took time to read stories to their children at night, followed by a prayer together. Bedtime is a sweet memory time for our family. We all four reminisce about the rough-housing "rompie" times with Dad, quiet moments of sharing, and loving prayers that brought us all close together at the close of each day. That extra effort was well-invested for the girls and for me. Being a "hands-off" rather than a hands-on parent now, I hold those memories very dear to my heart.

Harvest Time

Gardening, like parenting, brings a lot of joy. It is also a lot of work. I must say, hard work in our garden has paid off. We save the tough jobs for when the sun goes down. Rob is gracious to do the heavy tilling job as I gradually am adding more beds each year. Umm . . . nothing like freshly tilled black dirt just waiting to be planted! I can hardly wait till he is done to get my hands in it!

My master gardener friend Carmen gave me another rule of thumb: work in plenty of compost and mulch whenever you put in a new plant. The little guy has to be able to breathe! And use chemicals sparingly and only as a last resort. Many insect infestations can be dealt with by just a strong blast of water from the hose.

I liken that advice to the way we are to both love and chasten our children. A gardener does not just plant seeds and let them be. Parents, don't just give birth and leave the rest to chance. Children are the product of many experiences, genetics, nutrition, and certainly of their parents' love. To see them blossom to their fullest, we must "work in" all the ingredients a new seedling needs to survive.

Nature tells us so. A plant can never be

The energy and commitment it took to make bedtime memorable was well worth it!

successful at extending its roots downward without preparing and softening the soil. Pushing deep into the ground, the well-rooted plant will be strong and anchored — no matter what storms may threaten!

Free to Stay Home

For a mom, no endeavor is more satisfying than the freedom to stay home or devote time to a career. For me, mothering full-time was completely my own choice. I was prepared to choose it joyfully, mindful that I was taking myself out of the professional writing and speaking arena for 20 years. I was confident that the 20 years in the "unpaid" work force at home would pay off in my daughters' lives. It certainly did. Without reservation, Rob supported me in that decision. We were single-minded in this concern for the welfare of our children.

Hopefully, you have reached your own answers to those compelling questions. They are difficult choices to make. I encourage you to *be there* during the season of your little ones' lives when they need the most nurturing and physical care. The first five years are especially critical.

Contrary to what some want us to believe, thousands of moms out there are nodding in complete agreement. I've met them all over this country! Don't miss out on your child's childhood just because some television documentary says it won't matter. Raising your child is a job that really matters — no matter *what* degrees you may hold. By being home you not only get to be there for your child's milestones, but you are there to kiss those hurts *when they happen, affirm their esteem, applaud their achievements, and help them in the way of the Lord on a daily basis.*

I used to balk at the question, "And what do you do?" Dear moms, never answer with *"Oh, I'm just a wife and mother."* Mothering at home may not stash a big bank account, but the dividends you are investing will be reaping interest far after you're gone. The media sometimes portrays full-time parenting as unflattering and demeaning.

But, the young mothers I meet all across the land are thankful every day for the joy they are allowed to fulfill as a full-time mother. They are not a bunch of crazed, right-wing, brain-dead women. These are talented, educated, creative women who are using their gifts to their fullest potential in their current profession of motherhood. It's a decision each woman must make for herself. I encourage you to think about it very seriously.

Many women return part-time to the work force out of financial necessity within a few years after childbirth. Some have found creative ways to

Raising your child is a job that really matters.

supplement a second income in today's pressing economy. I applaud them! Have they lagged behind professionally? Perhaps a little, but they believe the tradeoffs have been well worth it.

It is impossible to over-estimate the value of a parent's love in a child's life. There is no adequate replacement. Children crave love much more than the lavish gifts any salary can provide.

Harvest Time

In just six short months I will sit in the pew reserved for "mother of the bride." I'll watch with misty eyes as the young woman in white in the rear of the church confidently grasps her father's arm and glides forward. I will be suddenly aware of the brevity of motherhood. "They" were right all along, you know. I will join the ranks of "they" who counseled me, "Treasure every minute. You'll blink and she will be grown."

For 23 years I nurtured, educated, and prayed, and now am bringing in the harvest . . . all to raise a child who, as an adult, would follow the leading of her Lord. God entrusted Rob and I with a precious gift. I'm glad I set that phase of my life apart for mothering responsibilities.

No, I am not an extraordinary mother . . . I lose my patience, get frustrated, and still am not exactly clear on what a "good" mother is. But, somewhere amidst the diapers, dishes, and duties . . . God worked little miracles every day in the hearts of a little girl and young mother.

And on her wedding day, I will have good reason to be proud of the precious little girl who has now become God's woman.

> To my mother, Lindy Baird:
> Your constant support, sacrifice, and love continually bring a calm and comfort to my heart. Yours and daddy's home is a little bit of heaven on earth I love to return to!

Invite a Miracle Into Your Home

Rob and I sat in shock listening, yet not really grasping the full impact of the evening's news report. One of the local news reporters was standing in front of a house just minutes from ours. It was as if our minds refused to comprehend the horror. In disbelief, we caught bits and pieces of the story. All four residents were dead. During the night the father had violently shot and killed his son, daughter, and wife; then held the gun to his own head.

Rob and I sat speechless. We didn't know the family personally, but had shopped in their gift store and the couple had waited on me personally. Several of my friends knew them well and had worked side

He is the happiest, be he king or peasant, who
finds peace in his home.
Johann Wolfgang Von Goethe (1749-1832)

Let us therefore follow after the things which
make for peace, and things wherewith one
may edify another
(Rom. 14:19;KJV).

by side with them in various jobs over the years. What intense discomfort and pain was present in that home that could drive a father to think death was his only remedy?

Even more poignant to me than seeing the bodies being carried one by one out of the house, was the house itself. Television cameras panned in closely to capture ruffled curtains at each window, potted mums in bloom, and a fall holiday wreath on the door. Its architecturally elegant, yet relaxed design combined to create the seemingly perfect aesthetic setting. I'd been down that street many times. Even "garage saled" with a friend at that very house.

How "normal" the house had seemed. American suburbia. Now it had become a murder scene. A house of affluence that looked quite content to the outside world had apparently been filled with some unseen resentment or smoldering anger for quite some time. I clipped the next morning's newspaper article for my journal. It's obvious message for me was loud and clear — the accumulation of pleasures, possessions, and power does not make a house a home of comfort!

Face it. You and I are afraid if we open the door of contentment, the unwanted guests of sacrifice and need will rush in. We've been led to believe that with the accumulating of "stuff" comes happiness. We're programmed to "get all you can" — whatever the sacrifice we have to make. We are made to feel ashamed if we don't keep up with the Joneses, or whatever names our neighbors might have.

Small wonder many of us stretch, strain, charge, and borrow in futile attempts to keep up a lifestyle that our culture claims is the "norm." Stop and think. Just about the time you think you have gotten all you need to be content, you begin to think you need something else. Or you observe that your friend has just gotten something better and bigger . . . whatever that "something" is . . . you fill in the blank!

We crave things that we don't need or enjoy. We buy things to impress others — people that we don't even know. Then we justify that we deserve something better. We must clearly understand that our insane attachment to possessions leads to feelings of inferiority and bondage. Not quite the life of comfort we'd like!

It took me a long time to learn to shout "No!" to indulgence. In my first year of marriage, I found myself in a shopping dilemma! Determined not to sacrifice my level of lifestyle, I opened my first credit card account. With those first purchases I felt so grown up! What a rush! I was in control! On my way to credit-card heaven!

The bill at the end of the month was a bit of a downer, but I didn't need to pay it all. I noted with growing interest (no pun intended) that the letter said I could finish paying next month. No big deal, then. Thoughts would cross my mind: You can't afford this!" I would tell myself, *If one plastic brings this much ecstasy, how much can I enjoy with more cards?* Answer: Get more cards!

I spent more. Rob and I both spent more. We also fought and

fretted more. Spending was in danger of becoming an addiction to replace the unhappiness and emptiness. It took more and more shopping sprees to provide the momentary feelings of power, control, and worth. There was always something new, something better out there to acquire. It was exhausting. All too soon, life came crashing down. We were deep in debt. We'd become enslaved to the things of this world.

That was over 25 years ago. I still remember how long it took to pay off all those bills. We began to be convicted about our spending. We drew up a rigid budget with the help of a financial counselor. For a long period of time we made up our own entertainment because we had no auxiliary spending. We learned what it was like to sit still before the Lord. We sought first the kingdom of God and his righteousness, and all the things that really mattered were added unto us (Matt. 6:33).

Life became simpler and far less complicated. All that "stuff" took too much time to care for anyway. We withdrew from the status race. One of the wonderful things about simplicity is its ability

The accumulation of pleasures, possessions, and power does not make a house a home of comfort!

to give contentment in the gracious provision of God. No longer did we have a love affair going on with the accumulation of possessions.

Instead of walking through my home looking at things that could use replacing, refurbishing, or refinishing, I began to walk through my home praising and thanking God for having such a lovely shelter in which to live.

Keeping my focus on the Lord rather than on stuff set me free! We were free from the bondage of this world's system and the "cravings of sinful man, the lust of his eyes and the boasting of what he has and does" (1 John 2:16).

If you find yourself discouraged and drowning in the stormy sea of financial debt, don't give up! At times, I make progress and then slip into old spending habits. That's a pattern for most of us in all areas of life, including finances. A correcting of our attitudes and actions keeps most of our desires in perspective. Remembering the stress and weariness that deep debt brought to my heart extinguishes the desire for foolish spending quicker than anything. "Better is little with the fear of the Lord than great wealth with turmoil" (Prov. 15:16).

That's the way it's got to be with you and me. When I really, really want something, God will give me the desire of my heart IF I "commit . . . to the Lord; trust in him" (Ps. 37:4-5). Notice the condition of committing and trusting. At times, the Lord allows me to have my heart's desires; other times He changes those desires. Still other times, He lets me wait and provides the financial means over time.

Whether in the state of wanting or the state of waiting, I can rejoice because I choose like Paul, "in whatsoever state I am, therewith to be content" (Phil. 4:11;KJV). Paul admits it's a learning process.

> Listen to Jesus: ". . . be content with your pay" (Luke 3:14).
> And to another apostle: ". . . not pursuing dishonest gain" (1 Tim. 3:8).

Now I warn you — it won't be easy. I don't mean to imply that at all. Contentment often requires marching out of step with others; being genuinely convinced that you are listening to the right drummer. That takes a miracle. It has nothing to do with the circumstances of life. It has everything to do with learning to trust a faithful God who can supply all your needs according to His riches in glory.

What comfort that kind of contentment can bring to your heart!

Do You Need a Miracle?

I have often found that I never truly appreciate something or some-one until it is taken away, even if for a short time. Personal posses-sions, health, my children, emotional peace . . . expectations. Some-how, I have to admit, I thought I would be exempt from life's catastro-phes. I guess I just assumed those were ugly realities that happened to everyone else. Not me.

Of course, I was wrong. Very wrong. Life is riddled with unexpecteds. Everyone wants to control their life. I used to think I could. With my day-timer and organizational skills in hand, I manage to control my life quite well, thank you. After all, aren't we told that the most successful and happiest people plot and plan?

Sometimes it takes something like "the flood of '93" that deluged all of Des Moines. It was the most costly disaster in Iowan history. Thousands of homes were destroyed in the devastation. Plans and in-vestments of many folks we know were reduced to rubble. I naively expected to come out of the experience unscathed. I expected to stay safe in my bed through the night. I expected to keep all my posses-sions. I expected to glide above troubled waters.

My expectations failed. Water swallowed the entire downstairs of our home. My treasure became trash. Over the rest of the summer my schedule was altered. Even the simplest of plans were affected without water, gas, or electricity and the time it took in long water lines those first weeks. Instead of being in control, I found myself groping for flashlights and buckets in the dark, learning firsthand what being "not in control" really means.

Control is a big issue for all of us. Being in control means that life would live up to my expectations. I'll be the first to admit this is a big issue for me. Attempting to control our own life (and others') is a trap we women fall into often, whether consciously or unconsciously. After all, when we're in control — kids obey, husbands are loving, and friends are supportive. Everyone jumps through our hoops. Right?

Not always so. No matter how well we manipulate to get control of our lives, those unexpecteds are going to come. Flood waters of frustration, helplessness, anger, and despair rush in at any moment. How strongly do you try to control your life? As a wife, do you manipulate using food, whining, sex, or guilt to control your husband? Do you use screaming, affection, and bribes to control your children and friends?

Are you experiencing a fearful flood right

I have learned, in whatsoever state I am, therewith to be content

(Phil. 4:11).

now? Perhaps you have just about drowned. You question if your life will ever seem "normal" again. You may be wondering if you are even going to survive — you're not so sure you even want to.

Is God still in the miracle-working business? You betcha! He alone is the sure Rock on whom we can stand when the floods of life come pouring in over life's shifting sands. We can sing, "On Christ the solid Rock I stand. All other ground is sinking sand." We can say with the Psalmist:

> God is our refuge and strength, an ever-present help in trouble. Therefore we will not fear, though the earth give way and the mountains fall into the heart of the sea, though its waters roar and foam and the mountains quake with their surging (Ps. 46:1-3).

It took me a while to understand, but I found Isaiah 43:2-3 to be a great comfort during the flooding:

> When you pass through the waters, I will be with you; and when you pass through the rivers, they will not sweep over you. . . . For I am the Lord your God.

Many homes and many lives badly need a miracle. Right now.

The family should be a closely knit group. The home should be a self-contained shelter of security; a kind of school where life's basic lessons are taught; a kind of church where God is honored; a place where wholesome recreation and simple pleasures are enjoyed.

Billy Graham (1918-)

And these words, which I command thee this day, shall be in thine heart: And thou shalt teach them diligently unto thy children, and shalt talk of them when thou sittest in thine house, and when thou walkest by the way, and when thou liest down, and when thou risest up

(Deut. 6:6-7;KJV).

Today. Let me show you what I've learned about miracles during another time of personal desperation. This time the only flood waters streaming were my tears. I came to realize my absolute inability to do anything and God's ability to do the miraculous.

Crash Landings

Unwittingly, I had assumed that since we raised our daughters in a godly home we would never face one of them straying spiritually. When I saw other parents and their children struggling, I'd wonder what those parents had done wrong. Now I view other parents and their children with compassion rather than judgment.

I rocked both of my daughters as infants, played hide and seek with them as toddlers, and walked them right up to the classroom door on their first day of school. For hours I sat on hard bleachers watching ball games, cheerleading, and school plays. I agonized over algebra and dating disappointments. I was there for the big moments, as well as the everyday, mundane moments. I invested so much providing the best protection, support, and love that I could.

And then I found out, I had to let them go! Release them! Cut the strings!

Off to college Missy and Mindy both flew — over a thousand miles away. When the fledgling, almost-adult child flies that far from the nest, it's inevitable that there will be some false starts — or some

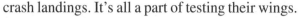

crash landings. It's all a part of testing their wings.

Our family survived the loneliness that first year the girls were gone. Rob and I grieved the part of our life that was over. After a couple of months we truly began enjoying our newfound relationship. Our empty nest was quickly turning into a love nest.

With the door of a whole new world opened up to her for the first time, Mindy reveled in being so far from home and parental authority. She had always been so strong in her love for God, that I was not worried. That is, at first.

I could tell within the first week of her junior year, Mindy was hurting. Over the phone the pain came through little by little even though she tried to cover it up with cheery bits of news and small talk. As we picked her up at the airport for Christmas break, my worst fears were confirmed. One look into her eyes told me what I'd only suspected and could not see through the phone wires.

A mama can see it in her own child's eyes. I couldn't miss the pain I saw. Mindy was a wounded, hurting young woman. Oh, how my heart ached for my daughter. I did not know what she had been through or where the pain was coming from, but the girl I took home from the airport

that day was not the same girl I had seen take off five months before.

Where Do You Take Broken Dreams?

I began to do what any loving mom would do. I prodded; I preached; I pleaded. That did a lot of good. Yeah, right.

I cried through much of the holidays. One day, looking for Christmas presents, I had to leave the store when Mindy came to mind. It was difficult for me to see her getting hard and hateful at times. She had always been such a sensitive, loving person. The more I saw Mindy hurting, the more I hurt. I did not know how to help or get her to open up. I felt squarely up against the one situation over which I had no answers and no control.

New Year's Day arrived with a bang — literally! Jolting me out of my journaling was the ring of our telephone. It sounded like a gun shot – and the message on the other end had an effect on me nearly as powerful. The voice on the other end identified himself as our local police. I had never received a call prefaced with that statement. (That's the call other parents get; so I thought.) He began with a question about an incident involving some young people on New Year's Eve. Our Mindy included.

My heart sank. When confronted the previous night she had reported having a "boring, quiet evening." What I was hearing from the officer did not sound either quiet or boring!

I tried to finish my coffee and goal-setting and re-committing, which was my custom on every other New Year's Day. I usually loved that yearly "clean slate," but on this New Year's morning, pain paralyzed me. No goal-setting for the year appeared on the blank paper before me. Only questions stared back.

What did I do wrong as a mom to make Mindy deliberately choose to walk down such a destructive road? Had I been too strict . . . too easygoing . . . expected too much . . . too little? How could a woman who goes all over the world teaching other women have an adult child living a lifestyle that does not affirm her teachings? Blaming myself had a way of trapping me in a rut that dug me deeper into a hole of despair.

During the next weeks my faith roller-coastered. Even as I comforted myself with the many times I had seen God answer prayer, I struggled under the horrendous doubts that He would do it again. I scoured my Bible for a promise to claim that could give me hope.

I came across the stories in the Bible where

They ran to Jesus for help.

Happiness is caused by things that happen around me, and circumstances will mar it; but joy flows right on through the dark; joy flows in the night as well as in the day; joy flows all through persecution and opposition. It is an unceasing fountain bubbling up in the heart; a secret spring the world can't see and doesn't know anything about. The Lord gives his people perpetual joy when they walk in obedience to Him.
Dwight Lyman Moody (1837-1899)

Rejoice in the Lord always; and again I say, Rejoice
(Phil. 4:4;KJV).

other parents were in need of a miracle for their child (Matt. 17, Mark 7, Luke 8, Mark 9). They all did the same thing. They ran to Jesus for help. Sometimes He healed immediately; other times the miracle was delayed. Jairus pleaded with Jesus to heal his daughter. The bystanders laughed at his pleas and said she was already dead. No use to trouble Jesus now. Jesus answered them that she was not dead, only sleeping.

That's it! Mindy's not gone yet! There's still hope! She's just asleep! Asleep to the truths that haven't awakened in her heart yet!

One evening Rob and I thought it might be a safe time to bring up our thoughts to Mindy. Boy, were we wrong! We tried to be kind and loving. Unwittingly, our words sounded self-righteous and judgmental. Alienated further, Mindy walked out during supper in a restaurant.

For 40 minutes I walked the mall searching in every shop for my daughter. Tears streaming down my face, I didn't care who I ran into. I just wanted to find Mindy. I wasn't sure if or when I'd ever see her again.

Finally, I spotted her at the mall entrance. No, she did not want a ride home. Yes, she had already called someone to come get her.

I fully expected to find her room cleared out when we arrived home. Rob caught up with me carrying the uneaten dinners in to-go boxes. We headed home to see what we'd find. Or not find.

Not knowing when (or if) Mindy was returning, I knelt beside the bed in her room to pray. It was all I knew to do. I could not carry my pain anymore. Sobbing, I buried my head in Mindy's pillow. I remember smelling her sweet scent and hugging that pillow like I longed to hug her.

I wanted a miracle just like the parents I had read about in the Bible. I knew I had to do what they did. Go straight to Jesus. That is just what I did. Like Jairus, I "fell at Jesus' feet, pleading with him to come to his house because his only daughter, a girl of about twelve, was dying" (Luke 8:41). Even when others thought the girl was too far gone and they "laughed him to scorn," Jairus kept pleading with Jesus to raise up his daughter. I did the same.

I didn't know what else to do.

I began by giving Him my fears, my pain, and my sorrow. As if they were a present, I verbally laid down my broken dreams and the expectations that I had for Mindy. Visually I wrapped them in beautiful paper and put a bow on top!

"Lord, she's yours, not mine," I prayed. "I fear the dangers of her lifestyle and what might happen, but she belongs to you. Not to me. You can take Mindy and do what You see best. I won't fight against You anymore. Please take hold of her hand like you did Jairus' and say, 'Arise.' Please revive Mindy, too!"

New Beginning

O God,
What shall I do?
I am at the total end
Of myself.
Wonderful, dear child!
Now start your new beginning
With me.

— Ruth Harms Calkin[3]

Comfort Comes Softly

Having given such a great sacrificial gift, I expected to feel sad and fearful of what might happen next. Instead, I felt lighter, happier than at any time since Mindy's return home. I had admitted the possibility of what I feared most. I had walked right up to my fear. And the result? The result was surprising: my fear was gone. By releasing Mindy to God, I released myself from responsibility. What happened to Mindy now was up to God.

Matthew 17 teaches that the faith for such a miracle cannot happen "but by prayer and fasting."

I knelt beside the bed in her room to pray.

Rob and I implored our immediate extended family to devote one day where Mindy would be prayed for during the next few months. We knew this was a critical time.

Every one of us emerged better, not bitter from those months. God's intention through all that was to drive us closer to himself, not farther from himself. I began to realize that God was working all things for my good, regardless of the outcome on Mindy's part. That was up to God.

One morning when Mindy got called in to work, I went to the counseling session in her place. (I knew we'd have to pay the fee for canceling too late anyway, so I figured it couldn't hurt.) His advice was like soft snow — it fell on my heart softly and sank in deeply. I was told just what I needed to hear. "Sharon, you are not responsible for Mindy's decisions. You are not the cause for what is going on right now, and you are not the cure."

That was good for me to hear. I was encouraged to keep loving and affirming to Mindy. So I did. Often a difficult task — especially on those days when I didn't feel like liking her, let alone loving her. I came to grips with the mistakes I made as a parent and sought Mindy's forgiveness. I found out that the words "I'm sorry" don't make a person choke after all. She graciously listened and forgave.

Softly, silently, God's comfort filled our home again. We did what Lamentations 2:19 says to do: "Pour out your heart like water in the presence of the Lord. Lift up your hands to him for the lives of your children."

We were encouraged from Scripture, expecting great things to happen. Those "things" didn't happen all at once. But, I began to realize our home was once again filled with an atmosphere of love and understanding. And even fun some days!

I learned to allow God to work in His timing. While waiting on Him, the Lord showed me that the attitudes I was allowing in my heart were as sinful as my daughter's rebellion. That broke me. All I could do was confess them, weep over them, and plead with God for cleansing and mercy. I stopped lecturing and criticizing her. Most importantly, I prayed and loved her. The miracle of comfort followed.

Oops! Too Much Lotion!

By taking off our guarded, concrete masks, all of us — Sharon, Rob, and Mindy began to release a smile or two. One day we got downright fanatical and laughed a big belly laugh over something silly at the supper table! That night I recorded the event in my journal! It was as if Jesus himself was infusing us with a sense of hope. "Relax!" He seemed to say lovingly, "There's not a thing wrong here that I can't take care of."

A few weeks after the restaurant incident, while I was rinsing the dishes one evening, Mindy came through the kitchen to chat. When I was done I dried my hands and poured out hand lotion. Way too much hand lotion. I held out my hand to see if Mindy wanted the excess. I will never forget those moments that followed.

I took her hands gently into mine and caressed them as if they were the soft fur of a kitten. For at least 30 seconds we soothed lotion into one another's hands.

In those tender moments, looking eyeball to eyeball at one another, we shared much more than hand lotion that day. It was a real turning point. In that simple gesture of only a few moments, it was as though the soothing balm of Gilead was being applied to our souls (Jer. 8). Not only our hands, but both of our hearts were soothed and softened.

God is able to heal hurts. Out of our admitted weaknesses — physical, mental, emotional, spiritual — can come His marvelous strength. Instead of our weakness being a hindrance, with God in charge, our weaknesses can enable His strength to flow through.

Any time our family uses hand lotion now, we always pour out a little extra. We turn to the nearest person and share! Even my mega mass of a husband! Rob used to think lotions were too "girly and gooey."

I expect to pass through life but once. If therefore, there be any kindness that I can show, or any good thing I can do to any fellow being, let me do it now, and not defer or neglect it, as I shall not pass this way again.
Stephen Grellet (1773-1855)

The days of our years are threescore years and ten; and if by reason of strength they be fourscore years, yet is their strength labour and sorrow; for it is soon cut off, and we fly away
(Ps. 90:10;KJV).

He even likes to get in on the group lotion lovin' now!

Want, Waive, Wait, Watch!

From the vantage point of nearly two years later, I can see how I was being forced to lie in green pastures by very still waters. When God wants to get your attention — He does it through those you love the most. In those pastures I:

WANTED A MIRACLE
WAIVED (RELINQUISHED) ALL RIGHTS AND ALL
    CONTROL
WAITED FOR A MIRACLE. God's timing is always best!
WATCHED GOD WORK!

Today Mindy is doing just fine. She is *so much more* than just fine! She's awesome! Serving on the staff of a great church for six months now, she is looking forward to starting work on her master's in counseling soon. God has done exceedingly abundantly more than I ever dared dream!

Do you need a miracle in your home? Maybe it isn't concerning a son or daughter. Maybe it concerns health, husband, finances, attitudes, betrayal, loss . . . whatever despair you are facing. Don't give up hope! Whenever you say something is hopeless, you slam shut the door of

God working a miracle. Let me encourage you to get back on the path of hope today!

And don't forget to stock up on some hand lotion. You're gonna need it!

With God in charge, our weaknesses can enable His strength to flow through.

Endnotes

1 Deniece Schofield, *Confessions of an Organized Housewife* (Cincinnati, OH: Better Way Books (div. of F & W Publishing, Inc., 1994).

2 Jill Richardson, "Steam Mad," *Christian Parenting Today*, Sept.-Oct. 1996, Vol. 9, No. 1, p. 26-28.

3 Ruth Harms Calkin, *Lord, It Keeps Happening and Happening* (Wheaton, IL Tyndale House Publishers, 1983).

About Our Cover Artist

Kit Hevron Mahoney has over 20 years experience as an artist and design professional. She was educated at the University of Colorado, Boulder, and at the Colorado Institute of Art in Denver, where she taught drawing and graphic design for 15 years. She was president/owner of Graphic Creations, Ltd., a national greeting card company and is now part owner of Abend Gallery Fine Art in Denver, where she shows her fine art. Since 1984, her watercolor and pastel landscape and floral paintings have been marketed through a variety of galleries and by private commission. Samples of her work can be viewed at http://home.earthlink.net/~kitm.